2019 SAGITTARIUS HOROSCOPE & ASTROLOGY

2019

Sagittarius

Horoscope & Astrology

Copyright © 2018 by Sia Sands

All rights reserved. This book or any portion thereof
may not be reproduced or used in any manner whatsoever without the express written permission
of the publisher except for the use of brief quotations in a book review.

The information accessible from this book is for informational purposes only. None of the data
within should be regarded as a promise of benefits, a statutory warranty or a guarantee of results
to be achieved.

Images are used under license from Dreamstime.

Acknowledgment:

Thank you to the stargazers, dreamers, and mystics.

You make this world a better place.

2019

Sagittarius

Horoscope & Astrology

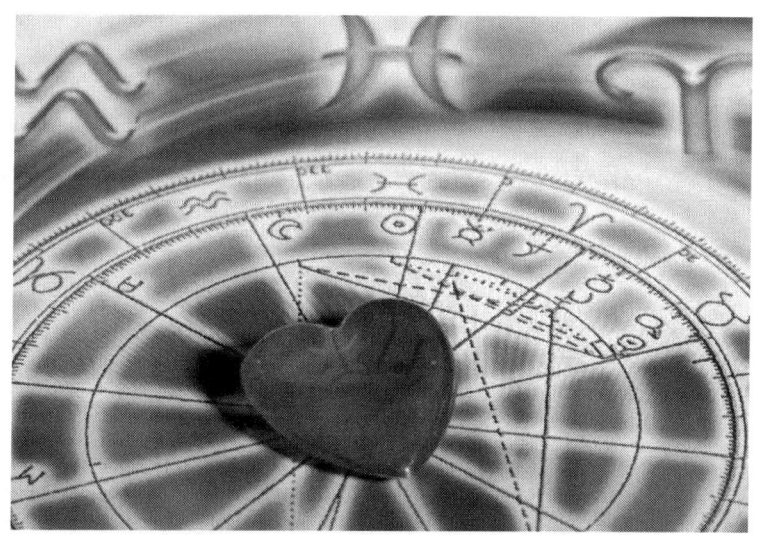

SAGITTARIUS 2019 OVERVIEW

Three powerful Supermoons arrive in the first few months of 2019, this ensures plenty of manifestation and healing comes in Sagittarius's life. This effect has an incredible ability to combine personal power with rejuvenation. The first two Supermoons are in Leo, which provides an extra boost for Sagittarius to distill into a blend which carries with it the potency of regeneration. The third Supermoon is a rare Blue Moon, and this brings mystical power into Sagittarius's spiritual life.

There are also hurdles to navigate with Mercury Retrograde leading Sagittarius into problematic places which Sagittarius usually doesn't have to face, this can cause unnecessary drama in Sagittarius's personal relations. Knowing what to watch out for is vital, Sagittarius has an impressive ability to restore lost equilibrium if mindful of the pitfalls, Sagittarius can take evasive action during Mercury Retrograde phases and prevent misunderstandings from snowballing into something much more significant.

2019 is a year of power and manifestation for Sagittarius. This dramatically expands Sagittarius's fire attributes. When harnessed correctly, Sagittarius can make remarkable progress towards developing their innovative ideas and real vision.

With many compelling reasons to embrace the year ahead, Sagittarius can look forward to harnessing brilliant cosmic energy to improve their personal potential throughout 2019.

JANUARY ASTROLOGY

January 1st – 5th - Quadrantids Meteor Shower.

The Quadrantids meteor shower run yearly from January 1st -5th. The Quadrantids meteor shower peaks on the night of the 3rd and morning of the 4th.

January 6th - New Moon in Capricorn.

This moon phase occurs at 01:28 UTC. This is an excellent time to star gaze as there is no moonlight.

January 6th - Venus with Greatest Western Elongation.

The planet Venus reaches it's highest eastern elongation of 47 degrees from the Sun.

January 6th - Partial Solar Eclipse.

This partial solar eclipse occurs in parts of eastern Asia and the northern Pacific Ocean.

January 14th – First Quarter Moon in Aries.

This Moon phase occurs at 06.45 UTC.

January 21ˢᵗ - **Full Moon in Leo.**

This full moon phase occurs at 05:16 UTC. This is known as the Full Wolf Moon because hungry wolf packs howled outside settlers camps. This full moon has also been identified as the Old Moon and the Moon After Yule.

January 21ˢᵗ - **Supermoon.**

This is the first of three super-moons for 2019.

January 21ˢᵗ - **Total Lunar Eclipse.**

This total lunar eclipse occurs in the majority of North America, South America, eastern Pacific Ocean, as well as the western Atlantic Ocean, extreme western Europe, and West Africa.

January 22ⁿᵈ - **Conjunction of Venus and Jupiter.**

A conjunction of Venus and Jupiter takes place with the two stunning planets within 2.4 degrees of each other in the pre-dawn sky.

January 27ᵗʰ – **Last Quarter Moon in Scorpio.**

This Moon phase occurs at 21.10 UTC.

JANUARY HOROSCOPE

JANUARY WEEK ONE

The past has a strong influence over you; it is part of a more significant phase, which currently runs through your life. Configuring your goals through the wisdom you have learned will take you to a bold new chapter. There are previous events which have triggered sensitivities, and this does take time to heal from. You are likely to reach a turning point soon as the opportunity is knocking and encouraging you to seek new potential. This disruptive energy is unsettling, you begin to see the situation through entirely new eyes. Be mindful of how you express yourself now, as it could lead to drama. Focus on re-balancing your energy will provide you with the best outlook. You turn a situation around this week.

The January 6th New Moon in Capricorn heals while it reveals new information.

JANUARY WEEK TWO

The past has been a valuable resource for growth and learning. Reflecting on the lessons learned, you can ascertain how you have reached this incredible level of wisdom. You are set to build on these foundations and release old and skewed insecurities which may flare up, this keeps you developing your creative path. As you resume a forward motion you clear away the fog and indecisiveness, you expand horizons and take on a challenging new role soon. You have an unusual ability to be able to understand people on a deeper level. Your gifts will lead you on a path which brings you great joy. You are set to make a great transition forward and can confidently move towards a new chapter this week. A moment of healing provides you with a valuable breakthrough.

The First Quarter Moon in Aries brings valuable information, this enables you to develop ambitious goals for the next phase of your vision. This adds a unique sense of promise to your life.

JANUARY WEEK THREE

The Super Full Moon in Leo is urging you to push out of your old comfort zone. You are drawing heightened social opportunities to you, this is likely to shake up potential and create a hotspot of opportunity. With a cluster of activity around the corner, you are set to benefit from networking with like-minded individuals. This leads to an expansive chapter which sees you hit it off with someone who is alluring and dynamic. This begins a necessary transition to a new chapter in your personal life. This one is focused and determined, they are an innovative, a distinctive person who has a strong sense of self. You are attracted to exploring life's mysteries with this individual, it does bring a great deal of opportunity into your world. Life is about to get a lot more interesting, as you expand your horizons, you draw in opportunities to achieve significant goals. News arrives soon, which provide you with a useful signpost. In fact, anything which is holding back your progress is released during the January 21st Total Lunar Eclipse.

JANUARY WEEK FOUR

Venus and Jupiter conjoin this week. Authoritative and compelling energy set to enter your life. You see yourself in a role which has you taking charge. Your leadership abilities hold you in good stead, and you can look forward to impressive results. This represents stability, ambition, authority, and achievement surrounding your world. You need to keep a calm head at this time and make decisions based on facts, not being overly influenced by emotions. You have been steadily reshaping your life, and are going to push to new levels of wisdom. You have learned some tough lessons in the past, but these have been crucial to providing you with the insight which currently helps move your life forward. You can feel very proud of your ability to make difficult decisions, and that you can be proactive about obtaining happiness. You can seize every opportunity you get to nurture yourself this week. An active person, you are likely to play an essential role in social events which arrive soon.

The January 27th Last Quarter Moon in Scorpio sees you take an impressive step towards achieving a vital goal on your unique path.

FEBRUARY ASTROLOGY

February 4th - New Moon in Aquarius.

This Moon phase occurs at 21:03 UTC. This is an excellent time to star gaze as there is no moonlight to obscure your view of the universe.

February 12th – First Quarter Moon in Taurus.

This Moon phase occurs at 22.26 UTC.

February 19th - Full Moon in Leo.

This Moon phase occurs at 15:53 UTC. The February full moon is known as the Full Snow Moon because the heaviest snows usually fall during February. As hunting was difficult, this full moon has also been recognized as the Full Hunger Moon.

February 19th - Supermoon.

This is the second of three Supermoons for 2019. The Moon will be at its nearest approach to the Earth and will look slightly larger and brighter than usual.

February 26th – Last Quarter Moon in Sagittarius.

This Moon phase occurs at 11.28 UTC.

February 27th - Mercury at largest Eastern Elongation.

The planet Mercury reaches an eastern elongation of 18.1 degrees from the Sun.

FEBRUARY HOROSCOPE

FEBRUARY WEEK ONE

There is a situation that needs balancing, taking all elements you spend time gaining insight into the path ahead. There may be delays which have caused frustrations, miscommunications and issues have dealt a blow. Using this time to tweak and revise your plans, you are given fresh inspiration which proves to be fruitful. You soon enter a chapter which holds great promise for emotional abundance to flow freely in your personal life. You are going to open new opportunities which provide you with a transition to a happier chapter. This helps you step into your own authority, you make smart decisions which provide you with broader options. You have been on a marathon of a journey to get this far, but you are now more likely to see tangible results flow into your world. Now, life begins to lighten, you can enjoy the flow of potential which tantalizes and delights your awareness.

FEBRUARY WEEK TWO

You are likely to be entering an extensive time, you could be feeling as though your energy is directed into many directions at once. Remember to pace yourself, prioritize, and focus on one area at a time. This will put you in good stead to handle the hectic pace of this week. You can release anxiety into the universe. Focus on the good and let the divine handle everything else. Things are set to enter a happier chapter soon. This sees you find an outlet for your restless energy, it does provide you with a useful area to develop. This is a time which allows you to make progress on your personal goals. It sets up an opportunity which will enable you to explore long-term goals. Keep setting those intentions, it does put you in a prime role of manifestation. Having an abundant mindset is vital in drawing new opportunities. You are entering a potent time which kicks off a fresh cycle of growth. This corresponds with making goals for the future and planning the strategic steps needed to stay on top of the game. This cycle also provides you with an adventurous time in your social life

FEBRUARY WEEK THREE

You are ready to engage in life, as several exciting avenues open up which see you participate more in a community setting. Invitations and events on the horizon all lead to an exciting time. Someone you meet and are with this week could play an especially important role in your life over the coming months. Your personal magnetism is supercharged, and you are likely to attract another individual's interest. Transformation sweeps in this week to encourage you to broaden your horizons, you can welcome change after spending a phase in introspection. This week plants the seeds for brilliant growth. A conversation you have soon is instrumental in providing you with a synergistic situation. This connection is likely to blossom the more involved you become with this person. You can take advantage of a dynamic new cycle and engage in lively encounters.

FEBRUARY WEEK FOUR

The planets align to provide you with extraordinary opportunities this week. Evaluating your larger goals will provide you with remarkable insight. Revamping your personal trajectory helps you make progress without repeating old patterns. You are richly creative and should share your brilliant ideas, especially with a broader audience. You have learned many lessons from the past and can put that wisdom to good use. You are self-confident and enthusiastic about your career. You seek to develop your path, and as you unfold this journey, you attract the influence of one who holds the key to growth. Your enthusiasm and exuberance for your goals are infectious. Your power is visionary, adaptable, and you transform the world around you with your vitality. You are on the path to a promotion, there is one who is watching your progress closely.

MARCH ASTROLOGY

March 5th – Mercury Retrograde begins in Pisces.

During a retrograde period, it isn't the right time to move forward in any practical venture. Be prepared for misunderstandings and miscommunications to be prevalent. You can make plans during this time, but it may be best to put them into action after the retrograde ends.

March 6th - New Moon in Pisces.

This phase occurs at 16:04 UTC. This is an excellent time to observe galaxies and stars because there is no moonlight to interfere.

March 14th – First Quarter Moon in Gemini.

This Moon phase occurs at 10.27 UTC.

March 20th - March Equinox.

The March equinox takes place at 21:58 UTC. The Sun be shining on the equator, and there will be equal amounts of day and night throughout the world. This is the first day of spring (vernal equinox) in the Northern Hemisphere.

March 21st - Full Moon in Libra, Supermoon.

This full Moon is on the opposite side of the Earth as the Sun and shall be adequately illuminated. This phase occurs at 01:43 UTC. This full moon is known as the Full Worm Moon because this is the time of year when the ground softens, and earthworms reappear. This full moon is also regarded as the Full Crow Moon, the Full Crust Moon, the Full Sap Moon, and the Lenten Moon. This is also the last of three super-moons for 2019.

March 28th - Last Quarter Moon in Capricorn.

This Moon phase occurs at 22.26 UTC. April 15 –

March 28th - Mercury Retrograde ends in Pisces.

You can now move forward with any delayed plans that you have been putting off due to the Mercury Retrograde phase. Relationships should soon improve as tensions ease.

MARCH HOROSCOPE

MARCH WEEK ONE

Growth and learning are the currency which brings success into your world. This is a time which suggests you engage in new activities and expanding your social environment. As you draw harmony, there is something familiar about the scene you find yourself in. Mingling with like-minded folk sweetly angles your spirit in a supportive manner. It is an inspirational and happy time ahead for you. Success sweeping into your word soon. Information brings opportunity knocking into your world. Keep your eyes open for news which stokes your imagination. A sense of telepathy flows between a manifestation and your mind. There is something brewing, this is leading you towards the realization of your goals. This surprise provides you with a positive boost. This is a beautiful time for self-development and beginning a practice of self-nurturing. This also enables you to heal old wounds and builds the right foundations for future growth.

MARCH WEEK TWO

You are especially sensitive to cosmic vibrations this week, the planet Mercury went into retrograde late last week, and you begin to feel some cosmic fallout. This is an essential time for restabilizing your life and letting go of energy which feels severe or heavy. You are a sensitive soul, and this can bring up strong feelings and emotions. There is some turbulence in your life which is likely to be released soon. Initially, this can bring sensitivities to the surface, taking time to reflect on the process brings deeper emotions which provides you with extensive opportunities for healing. This is a considerable investment in your well-being, you receive stabilizing energy which enables you to bring long-term thinking, structure, and stability into your life. You will soon be enjoying the harvest of the bounty which is a result of all the hard work you have put forth recently. The seeds you have planted continue to grow and create positive developments for you. You may find yourself rewarded, keep applying yourself diligently with the faith that those in charge appreciate the results you produce. They will provide you with a reward which allows you positive feedback.

MARCH WEEK THREE

You have been through a lot recently with Mercury retrogrades disruptive influence and can expect improvement to your circumstances this week. You are in a time of reflection. Unresolved feelings may arise which leave you feeling unsettled. You soon enter a phase of healing and closure, this enables you to process past events, and it leads to your next life chapter. This week marks an important beginning and helps you make a convincing transition forward. As you move ahead, something which no longer is needed is left behind so that you can confidently make strides towards achieving a happier chapter. This does spark heightened potential which moves into your world soon with a flourish. Reflecting on the past enables you to appreciate how precious this journey has been. It has given you a sense of wisdom and personal accomplishment. Your current situation spotlights a desire to expand your horizons. A trailblazing idea leads to an innovative path which is likely to become a high point in your life. The future brings exceptional moments in your life. Dealing with unprocessed emotions will provide you with valuable healing

MARCH WEEK FOUR

You see how far you have grown on your journey. You can be proud of the way you overcome hurdles and maintain an optimistic outlook. You are committed to improving your circumstances, and this will hold you in good stead as you move forward. You have a beautiful, idealistic nature and will bring golden moments into your surroundings. You are exceptional and highly creative. The past contains many treasured memories for you. It has had an impact on your current stage of personal development. As you reflect on the changes which currently surround your life, you will have a more significant epiphany of how much you have accomplished on your journey so far. A flood of inspiration returns into your world, and this takes you to a vibrant chapter which heralds abundant potential arriving to expand your horizons.

APRIL ASTROLOGY

April 5th - New Moon in Aries.

This moon phase occurs at 08:51 UTC. This is an excellent time to observe galaxies and stars because there is no moonlight visible.

April 11th - Mercury at most substantial Western Elongation.

The planet Mercury reaches its most substantial western elongation of 27.7 degrees from the Sun.

April 12th – First Quarter Moon in Cancer.

This Moon phase occurs at 19.06 UTC.

April 19th - Full Moon in Libra.

The Moon is on the opposite side of the Earth as the Sun and will be completely illuminated. This moon phase occurs at 11:12 UTC. This full moon is known as Full Pink Moon because it marks the appearance of the first spring flowers. This full moon has also been identified as the Sprouting Grass Moon, the Growing Moon, and the Egg Moon. Many coastal areas call it Full Fish Moon because this was the time the fish swam upriver to breed.

April 22nd, 23rd - Lyrids Meteor Shower.

The Lyrids meteor shower runs each year from April 16-25. This meteor shower peaks on the night of the 22nd and the morning of the 23rd. These meteors sometimes produce bright dust trails that last for several seconds.

April 26th – Last Quarter Moon in Aquarius.

This Moon phase occurs at 22.18 UTC.

APRIL HOROSCOPE

APRIL WEEK ONE

Going within enables you to find a place of quiet within your heart, this provides you with the intuition required to make a choice. Having faith that you can plan correctly enables you to achieve a high result. Taking an alternate approach may be crucial in this situation, rejecting old ways and discarding that which no longer works, enables you to achieve a complete turnaround. Expanding your understanding of your goals plays a significant role here. This week marks a time of surrender and letting go of that which has not reached fruition. It is a time of repose, waiting for further developments. As you reflect on the situation at hand, you will gain the wisdom necessary to make a decisive choice. This brings you to a happier phase and does provide you with the positive changes you have been needing Trusting in your higher self and destiny is part of this process.

APRIL WEEK TWO

You are heading towards a happier chapter. This is set to be a joyous season for you where you can enjoy the festivities and spend time with your inner circle. Being with people you feel comfortable letting your guard down around does draw valuable well-being into your world. You are a sensitive and creative person who nurtures friendships. Honoring your spirit helps guide your path forward correctly. You are headed to an area which offers robust potential, it enables you to carve out a niche which is perfect for you. Your expertise will be valuable to others, your inspiration is fueled by a desire to make a difference, your idealism and motivation run high. This enables you to focus on achieving substantial goals

Furthermore, an invitation arrives to entice you to engage more with your social life. It leads to a happy time where you connect with others who energize and enliven your life. Heightened activity is hectic but also welcomed as it increases the level of fun with kindred spirits. It is an entertaining and enjoyable week ahead.

APRIL WEEK THREE

The Full Moon in Libra appearance to inspire and motivate you this week. Your imagination is humming with new potential. This symbolizes the seeds of an idea that you feel excited about arriving to give you a new project to contemplate. There is a great deal of creative energy indicated for you this week, it is an extremely beneficial time to plan for future endeavors. This incredible energy holds within it the force of strength and enthusiasm. There are a few twists and turns as you navigate the week ahead, you may find some rearranging is required in your life to create an organized approach which will enable you to deal with a busy time ahead. You enter an extensive time which denotes a hectic schedule is around the corner. As your optimism picks up steam, you can also look forward to a solid phase ahead which sees you mingling with others.

APRIL WEEK FOUR

Clearing the air with another sees the potential is restored and bonds are renewed. Healing a rift sweeps into your life this week. This is a time of heightened communication, invitations arrive which leave you feeling upbeat and generous. You are ready to enjoy a social phase which sees you connecting well with other kindred spirits. Clarity arrives to point the way to another destination which may come as a surprise at first. You are being guided to think outside the box, expand your horizons, and achieve fabulous results. You feel encouraged you to be bold and harness the power of self-expression and creativity. There is a creative spark which seeks expression in your world. Something new is on the way, you are able to nurture and manifest a pleasant situation to fruition. This is a time which represents growth, prosperity, and happy conclusions. It is suggestive of potential being fulfilled in your world soon.

MAY ASTROLOGY

May 4th - New Moon in Taurus.

This phase occurs at 22:46 UTC. The new moon phase is a brilliant time to observe galaxies and stars because there is no moonlight visible.

May 6th, 7th - Eta Aquarids Meteor Shower.

The Eta Aquarids meteor shower runs annually from April 19 to May 28. It peaks this year on the night of May 6 and the morning of the May 7.

May 12th – First Quarter Moon in Leo.

This Moon phase occurs at 01.12 UTC.

May 18th - Full Moon in Scorpio, Blue Moon.

The Moon is on the opposite side of the Earth as the Sun, and its face will be fully illuminated. This phase occurs at 21:11 UTC. The May full moon is known as the Full Flower Moon because this is when spring flowers are in abundance. This full moon is also known as the Full Corn Planting Moon and the Milk Moon. This year it is also a blue moon. This unusual calendar event only happens once every few years, giving rise to the term, "once in a blue moon." There are usually three full moons in each season. A fourth full moon is called a Blue moon and occurs on average once every 2.7 years.

May 26th - Last Quarter Moon in Aquarius.

This Moon phase occurs at 16.33 UTC.

MAY HOROSCOPE

MAY WEEK ONE

The energy flowing toward you is nurturing, abundant, creative, and versatile. This nourishes your spirit and enhances your life on multiple levels. It encourages you to harness your sense of adventure and to engage in areas of your life that radiate vibrant potential. You are doing the right thing in reaching for substantial goals. You are on a path which will provide you with tangible results. Having faced and overcome many difficulties in your past history, you have a tenacious outlook which is able to provide you with valuable solutions. Your inner strength and fortitude have only increased as time goes by, you are someone others look up to. You are one who nurtures others and can embrace happy times ahead.

MAY WEEK TWO

You can expect a significant improvement soon. You are an excellent source of support to another. It is also essential to take care of your own needs, scheduling in some important self-care does help you on many levels. Following your heart, you stir up an abundant mindset. This draws well-being into your life, a project is coming which allows you to spread your wings, it brings you to a time of learning a new area. You can feel positive about the possibilities which surround your life this week. You are an honest and optimistic person who has a terrific approach to life. Whatever challenges you come across, you get through them and bounce back stronger than ever. Your deep love of the past is especially something to treasure. You respect tradition, and someone close can see themselves in you in so many ways. You will also find new ways to creatively express yourself to another soon.

MAY WEEK THREE

A rare Blue Full Moon occurs in Scorpio this week. This opens the gates to a busy and hectic time. Advancement is in the pipeline, you could get involved in a new initiative which provides you with a wealth of opportunities. One thing that is for sure, you can prepare for more action, organizing and streamlining is highlighted as being important. You see lovely expensive energy flow into your career sector this week. The beneficial effect of this time is likely to flow into next month as well. It provides you with recognition and has a direct impact on moving your career aspect forward. You should see movement around professional projects which have been stalled or have had setbacks in the past. This ignites new potential, as exclusive offers may also arrive to expand your horizons. This is a beautiful week for creating change

MAY WEEK FOUR

You have an incredible ability to stay true to yourself. You are ready to mark a bold new chapter in your personal life. This could see a situation changing or evolving, it spotlights something which has you moving in a direction which is in alignment with your own vision. You have a high capacity to mend situations, as your kindness is a beautiful part of your personality. Your creativity is going to hold you in good stead, keep forging ahead with your dreams. Favorable skies will reward your diligent efforts, your self-discipline is going to lead you to an opportunity which is advantageous. As you keep working on developing your talents, you uncover a hidden gift which takes you on the road less traveled. Releasing limiting beliefs helps draw abundance into your world.

JUNE ASTROLOGY

June 3rd - New Moon in Gemini.

This moon phase occurs at 10:02 UTC. This is an excellent time to observe galaxies and stars because there is no moonlight to interfere.

June 10t – First Quarter Moon in Virgo.

This Moon phase occurs at 05.59 UTC.

June 10th - Jupiter at Opposition.

The planet Jupiter will be at its nearest approach to Earth, and its planet face will be illuminated entirely by the Sun.

June 17th - Full Moon in Sagittarius.

The Full Moon is on the opposite side of the Earth as the Sun, and its face will be completely illuminated. This moon phase occurs at 08:31 UTC. This full moon is known as Full Strawberry Moon because it is the peak of strawberry harvesting season. The June Full Moon has also been identified as the Full Rose Moon and the Full Honey Moon.

June 21st - June Solstice.

The June solstice occurs at 15:54 UTC. The North Pole will be tilted toward the Sun, which, having reached its northernmost position in the sky will be over the Tropic of Cancer at 23.44 degrees north latitude. This heralds the first day of summer (summer solstice) in the Northern Hemisphere, and is considered one of the most influential times of the year for many traditional cultures.

June 23rd - Mercury at largest Eastern Elongation.

The planet Mercury reaches most substantial eastern elongation of 25.2 degrees from the Sun.

June 25th – Last Quarter Moon in Aries.

This Moon phase occurs at 09.46 UTC.

JUNE HOROSCOPE

JUNE WEEK ONE

You are likely to succeed in an innovative area which also harnesses the power of traditional methods. This provides you with an opportunity to get involved with a social group and helps you organize beneficial changes in your world. You enter a happier time soon which allows opportunities for self-expression. It all leads to a sense of well-being and balance. You can expect a myriad of opportunities to flow into your world this week. This allows you to take advantage of a time which offers heightened benefits for socializing. It brings a strong sense of balance into your home life. Focusing on family ties becomes a priority, this brings harmony into your world. It is a week of heightened self-expression, social engagement, and fun activities. An invitation to an event towards weeks end brings humor and joy into your surroundings. News also arrives from a close source which gives your life a boost.

JUNE WEEK TWO

The planet Jupiter reaches its closest approach to the earth this week. This week offers you heightened clarity and insight into the path ahead. A brilliant idea arises to entice you to try developing a new area. As you expand and broaden the potential in your life, you engage in energetic and creative thinking. It is a time of heightened perception, strategic planning, and dynamic thought processes. Developing ideas, changing direction, and rejecting outworn modes of being all lead to a compelling phase of potential. You seek out dynamic opportunities. Collaborating with innovative people will offer you a chance to develop your skill set. The universe is giving you the green light to embark on an area which provides growth and learning. This is a valuable time to nurture your talents as an innovative area is beckoning to be developed. Important news also arrives, which gives you a welcome boost.

JUNE WEEK THREE

You deal with a hectic time this week, you should channel your energy into carefully selected directions, this will allow you to avoid scattering your precious energy everywhere, it enables you to improve productivity and focus on areas which hold the most significant meaning to you. There is a great deal of abundance set to arrive for you. Essential changes coming, you find that you are ready to let go of drama and frustration. This brings new potential into your world, you move away from power struggles, conflicts, and limiting beliefs around emotional security. Your vision gains forward momentum, and this does suggest you seek happiness where you find it. You enter an energizing time which sees you prioritize on building a happier foundation in your life.

JUNE WEEK FOUR

This week show a significant situation deepens for you. You are an inspiration to others, you are someone who has a gift of empathy. Your love of justice makes you a natural advocate and campaigner for change. As you open people's minds to new concepts, you spread an optimistic message which makes the world a better place. Your talents will shine in a new role which is coming your way soon. Watch for divine signs which encourage you to expand your horizons rapidly. You can embrace a chapter which has you learning a new area. Taking time to reflect on the past does bring you valuable wisdom. You are entering a time of transformation, and you can expect creative solutions to help guide your path forward.

JULY ASTROLOGY

January 1st – 5th - Quadrantids Meteor Shower.

July 2nd - New Moon in Cancer.

This moon phase occurs at 19:16 UTC. This is an excellent time to observe galaxies and stars because there is no moonlight visible.

July 2nd - Total Solar Eclipse.

The total solar eclipse occurs in parts of the southern Pacific Ocean, central Chile, and central Argentina. A partial eclipse is visible in the Pacific Ocean and western South America.

July 7th – Mercury Retrograde begins in Leo.

During a retrograde period, it isn't the right time to move forward in any practical venture. Be prepared for misunderstandings and miscommunications to be prevalent.

July 9th – First Quarter Moon in Libra.

This Moon phase occurs at 10.55 UTC.

July 9th - Saturn at Opposition.

The beautiful ringed planet Saturn will be at its nearest approach to Earth, and it will be illuminated by the Sun.

July 16th - Full Moon in Capricorn.

The July Full Moon is located on the opposite side of the Earth as the Sun and will be fully illuminated. This phase occurs at 21:38 UTC. This full moon is known as Full Buck Moon because the male buck deer start to grow new antlers. This full moon is also known as the Full Thunder Moon and the Full Hay Moon.

July 16th - Partial Lunar Eclipse.

The partial lunar eclipse will be visible throughout most of Europe, Africa, central Asia, and the Indian Ocean.

July 25th – Last Quarter Moon in Taurus.

This Moon phase occurs at 01.18 UTC.

July 28th, 29th - Delta Aquarids Meteor Shower.

The Delta Aquarids meteor shower peaks on the night of July 28 and morning of July 29.

July 31st - Mercury Retrograde ends in Cancer.

You can now move forward with any delayed plans that you have been putting off due to the Mercury Retrograde phase. Relationships should soon improve as tensions ease.

JULY HOROSCOPE

JULY WEEK ONE

A decision is required to enable future progress to occur. As you gain a more comprehensive perspective, you realize that fear has been holding you back. You instinctively know that you desire to develop your dreams, even if that means veering out of your safety zone. This implies the need to go beyond your current comfort level and open yourself up to new opportunities which are available to you. Your creativity is strengthened as you acknowledge you have the courage to face trials, and you bravely open yourself to new possibilities. You radiate enriching creative potential. Become a channel for this new energy to enter your life, as it is in the balance with your emotions, inspirations, creativity, and ideas. You are set to benefit from a chapter which is emotionally rewarding, and this takes you to a happier place.

JULY WEEK TWO

You are strong, you have determination and willpower within you which is allowing you to achieve your goals, one step at a time. You come from a long line of enterprising innovators, you are shining in the role you find yourself in. You have high strength and adaptability. You have lovely gifts which can be channeled and create impressive results in your life. It is set to be a busy and productive week for you. You enter a phase which draws beneficial people into your world, opportunities to mingle see you networking with others. It provides you with a welcome sense of possibility as you enjoy sharing your ideas with others. It lights up a sense of abundant communication, you may also hear exciting and long-awaited news soon. This corresponds with getting back in touch with someone special.

JULY WEEK THREE

This week indicates that you are headed towards a happier chapter, this sees you surrounded by a vibrant crew of kindred spirits and positive thinkers. Your social life is warm and abundant. It connects you to someone who turns out to be a fascinating individual. These changes stoke your world for the better, it puts a spotlight on increasing emotional harmony and illuminates a chapter of passion, self-expression, and romance. The news is going to arrive which will help lift your spirits. You've had your challenges this year, but with your tough and tenacious spirit, you can improve your circumstances. While the complete answer may not completely arrive just yet, you will experience improvement over the coming month. Significant changes occur, this takes you to an exceptional phase which heralds a new flow of energy into your world. Additionally, invitations to social events entice you to change up your everyday routine. It could also bring a new friendship into your sphere, things continue to keep looking promising.

JULY WEEK FOUR

Taking a step back enables you to observe a broad perspective. This allows you to see a path which is going to provide you with long-term growth. There will be a calming weekend ahead where you are given the opportunity to set intentions and think about future goals. As you begin to put your vision into motion, you enter a cycle which sees you accomplish a great deal of growth. This is a strong time and the actions you take soon become the icing on the cake. Don't get drawn into the drama caused by others over this time; things will work out best this way. There are times when people touchy and out of sorts, this shouldn't be taken personally, they have the issues and not you. Keeping optimistic sends out the right type of energy to draw well-being into your world. Additionally, a specific opportunity arrives to provide you with a bonus if you make a snap decision.

AUGUST ASTROLOGY

August 1st - New Moon in Leo.

This moon phase occurs at 03:12 UTC. This is an excellent time to observe galaxies and stars because there is no moonlight to interfere.

August 7th – First Quarter Moon in Scorpio.

This Moon phase occurs at 17.31 UTC.

August 9th - Mercury at most substantial Western Elongation.

The planet Mercury reaches greatest western elongation of 19.0 degrees from the Sun.

August 12th, 13th - Perseids Meteor Shower.

The Perseids meteor shower runs each year from July 17 to August 24. It peaks this year on the night of August 12 and the morning of August 13.

August 15th - Full Moon in Aquarius.

The August Full Moon is located on the opposite side of the Earth as the Sun and will be fully illuminated. This phase occurs at 12:30 UTC. The August full moon is known as the Full Sturgeon Moon because sturgeon fish of the Great Lakes and other major lakes are plentiful. This full moon has also been identified as the Green Corn Moon and the Grain Moon.

August 23rd – Last Quarter Moon in Taurus.

This Moon phase occurs at 14.56 UTC.

August 30 - New Moon in Virgo.

This moon phase occurs at 10:37 UTC. This is an excellent time to view galaxies and stars because there is no moonlight to interfere.

AUGUST HOROSCOPE

AUGUST WEEK ONE

This is a special time for you, and as you make space to reflect on the changes which have arrived in your life this year, you can process some of the heavy emotions and deal with releasing outworn energy. This creates space for a fresh flow of abundance to enter your world. You can take advantage of an opportunity which arrives to tempt you on a diverse path. A spotlight is shining on improving your well-being, this inspires you to make changes which focus on self-development and can enable you to move forward through the busy time ahead with a sense of peace within your spirit. Seeking a better balance in your life is going to pay valuable dividends. A welcome surprise is around the corner for you.

AUGUST WEEK TWO

You have a penchant for overthinking things, and this can create barriers which limit your potential. Contrary to your preconceptions, you highly talented and able to surmount the highest obstacles with ease. Starting to question long-held beliefs helps release ingrained messages which could be preventing you from reaching your most certain destination. Doing this inner work helps amplify your gifts and improve your chances of success. You are ready to tackle your dreams. You have a tendency to put things on the back burner and put others needs first. You are soon likely to enter a phase which is transforming your awareness onto areas which highlight self-development and creativity. This week says it's high time you put yourself first and enjoyed developing a field which brings you joy.

AUGUST WEEK THREE

You are ready to work on building a stable platform from which to create the next chapter of your life. The potential for romance, creativity, and personal expression is set to soar in your life. You deepen a situation with someone who holds the key to the next phase of happiness in your world. You are likely to take a big-picture view at this time, in the long run, you will look back and see you have built a rock-solid foundation. You are finding yourself having to restart on many levels, this burns creativity brightly in the background. This power is going to help you create a stable platform from which to grow your talents. It takes you to a time of serious self-expression. You have been busy strengthening your sense of self-worth by going after personal goals and visions. Learning how to stand up for your own needs will be the ticket to success. You are likely to enter a phase which has you reaching for challenging solo projects and endeavors. These initiatives will bring you to an abundant chapter which holds promise.

AUGUST WEEK FOUR

You are entering a bountiful time which sets the stage for grand plans to be put in place. As you power ahead towards the realization of goals, you find life becomes more efficient, it leads to a breakthrough which beckons a new area to develop. You have impressive talents, keep evolving and sharing your expect expertise with others. A venture you engage in this week will flourish, as prosperity and abundance are at the foundation of this efficient energy. As your life becomes more secure, you can develop broader goals in your life, leading you towards greater prosperity. You have a sound mind for business, and combined with your cleverness, it will take you in an innovative area.

SEPTEMBER ASTROLOGY

September 9th - Neptune at Opposition.

The giant blue planet will be at its closest approach to Earth, and its face will be illuminated by the Sun.

September 6th – First Quarter Moon in Sagittarius.

This Moon phase occurs at 03.10 UTC.

September 14th - Full Moon in Pisces.

The September full Moon is on the opposite side of the Earth as the Sun, and its face will be fully illuminated. This phase occurs at 04:34 UTC. This full moon is known as the Full Corn Moon because the corn is harvested around this time. This full moon is also called the Harvest Moon which is the full moon that occurs nearest to the September equinox each year.

September 22nd – Last Quarter Moon in Gemini.

This Moon phase occurs at 02.41 UTC.

September 23rd - September Equinox.

The 2019 September equinox occurs at 07:50 UTC. The Sun shines directly on the equator, creating equal amounts of day and night throughout the world. This is also the first day of fall (autumnal equinox) in the northern hemisphere and is considered a significant zodiac event for many cultures.

September 28th - New Moon in Virgo.

This phase occurs at 18:26 UTC. This is an excellent time to observe galaxies and stars because there is no moonlight visible.

SEPTEMBER HOROSCOPE

SEPTEMBER WEEK ONE

Excitement and imagination figure prominently in this bright and a lively week. You find your goals become clearly defined, this gives you a prominent sign that you are on the right path. You engage in robust communications with someone who inspires your mind. This character emphasizes an intelligent mind and is more practical than most, able to lend a hand with everyday concerns. It is apt to be a highly unusual week which may even lean to the unconventional. It all brings a sparkle to your world. You have gifts of an entrepreneurial nature, broadening your horizons will break you through to a new area to develop. It's best not to be in a rush, explore your more full vista to your heart's content, enjoy the creative process and you will know which area to focus on.

SEPTEMBER WEEK TWO

The planet Neptune is at its closest approach to Earth this week, it will be at its brightest, this really gets the creative juices flowing for you. You can surmount any obstacle with your optimistic and tenacious outlook. You are headed towards a happier chapter, this will see you enter a time of growth and personal initiatives. Keep forging ahead with plans, the good news is coming, favorable skies will light your life. You are undergoing a significant transformation during this time. You have the power of manifestation is within you during this time. Considerable change is arriving, and this heralds a chapter which is empowering, forthright, and powerful. It is advised to keep a calm head at this time, make decisions based on facts, and not be overly influenced by emotions. This is a critical phase which will allow you to make progress in your goals. It also suggests a fair and reasonable influence is affecting your energy.

SEPTEMBER WEEK THREE

Focusing on staying balanced will enable you to take advantage of a new phase. It brings order to be chaotic parts of your spirit and does carry an intense bonding moment into your life. Creating sustainable plans leads to a stress-free environment which will hold you in good stead soon. You have had disruptive energy with you which suggests the influence of recent events is creating a chaotic environment around you. The good news is that it allows outworn energy to be released and it does make room for something new and unusual to follow. The past has been a time of massive growth, you may have found it a struggle to deal with sudden and rapid change which has occurred. There are many positives available to you currently, you can expect a surprise which shakes up potential and provides you with a welcome boost. This is an epic time for embracing heightened social opportunities, intimate encounters and gatherings with friends to bring you joy.

SEPTEMBER WEEK FOUR

The Equinox this week indicates growth opportunities arriving soon. Your personal life symbolizes fullness and fertility, there is a potency which suggests a new beginning is available. This unfolds and transforms your potential toward a meaningful situation. As you unfurl your dreams, you can nurture the love and affection of another who holds your attention. An aspiration you hold is about to be realized or the beginnings, a new love relationship is indicated for you. This stirs in your spirit wonderful feelings of excitement. The tides are turning so you can get ready for a decisive shift which brings higher love potential into your world. A person arrives to expand your horizons. This leads to an exciting opportunity to develop a closer bond. It highlights social interactions and the arrival of exciting news. You enjoy sharing ideas and thoughts with this charismatic individual. It does bring you to a chapter of change and potential.

OCTOBER ASTROLOGY

October 8th - Draconids Meteor Shower.

The Draconids meteor shower runs annually from October 6-10 and peaks this year on the night of the 8th.

October 5th – First Quarter Moon in Capricorn.

This Moon phase occurs at 16.47 UTC.

October 13th - Full Moon in Aries.

The October full Moon is on the opposite side of the Earth as the Sun, and its face will be fully illuminated. This phase occurs at 21:09 UTC. This full moon is known as the Hunters Moon because at this time of year the leaves are falling, and game animals are plentiful. This full moon is also known as the Travel Moon and the Blood Moon.

October 20th - Mercury at Greatest Eastern Elongation.

The planet Mercury reaches greatest eastern elongation of 24.6 degrees from the Sun.

October 21st – Last Quarter Moon in Cancer.

This Moon phase occurs at 12.39 UTC.

October 21st, 22nd - Orionids Meteor Shower.

The Orionids meteor shower runs yearly from October 2 to November 7. Orionids meteor shower peaks this year on the night of October 21 and the morning of October 22.

October 27th - Uranus at Opposition.

The planet Uranus will be at its nearest approach to Earth, and its face will be illuminated by the Sun.

October 28th - New Moon in Scorpio.

This moon phase occurs at 03:39 UTC. This is an excellent time of the month to view galaxies and stars because there is no moonlight visible.

October 31st – Mercury Retrograde begins in Scorpio.

During a retrograde period, it isn't the right time to move forward in any practical venture. Be prepared for misunderstandings and miscommunications to be prevalent.

OCTOBER HOROSCOPE

OCTOBER WEEK ONE

Flexibility, empathy, and compassion will allow you to overcome challenges. You have a right to feel frustrated by recent events, it does provide you with an opportunity for personal growth which can be downright empowering if utilized correctly. Curveballs do unbalance you, but how are you ultimately react is critical. You are going to enter time which allows you to make adjustments, being mindful of the complexities of situations around you, enable you to progress forward in a balanced fashion. This allows the energy to bring harmony into your world instead of fueling issues. Hidden information could come to light which provides you with a path forward. An opportunity to repair a bond arrives, which enables a misunderstanding to be overcome.

OCTOBER WEEK TWO

You have been dealing with a lot this year, this has left you having to completely reorganize your life and change many goals. You have had to become more confident, and bold as it has taken a great deal of swift action and decisiveness to reach this point. You may be feeling torn about the past, but you mustn't have regrets, you have always shone brightly, even under stressful circumstances. Watch for a sign which has you looking back to the past. Some clues will guide you towards a time which provides you with healing. You explore ways of easing burdens through sharing your experiences with another. You are set to be inspired by developing innovative projects which are close to your heart. The winds of change sweep into your life and will add light to your life.

OCTOBER WEEK THREE

Your past has been a rich tapestry which has provided you with many answers. It will pay off in your current situation, as the wisdom you have gained is beneficial in developing your goals. You find you are attracting the attention of another soon. This suggests you should share your feelings with them. You are reading to make some changes, planning to build stable foundations, you seize the opportunity to put yourself out in new situations. This leads to leisurely social encounters, and it allows your spirit to re-calibrate and rejuvenate. It brings you in contact with a valuable mentor. You build foundations correctly which provides you with increased stability. Allowing your curiosity to guide you, you step out of the box to make the most of this enterprising influence.

OCTOBER WEEK FOUR

The planet Uranus will be at its closest approach to Earth this week. There soon will be powerful opportunities to connect with like-minded people. This is perfect timing, it brings you in touch with creative kindred souls who form the basis of your more full circle of friendships. It is an indulgent time of serendipity, it conjures a wonderful feeling of well-being and harmony. As your social life brings you joy, you feel drawn towards developing a closer bond with another. There are indications that refreshing changes will be emerging in your life, this sparks an artistic and creative phase, allow your urges to guide you, your passions are encouraging you to expand your horizons. This unstoppable original drive is heading full force towards an exciting new endeavor. You may feel especially vibrant and radiant. A situation in your social sector also is highlighted as drawing abundance to you.

NOVEMBER ASTROLOGY

November 4th – First Quarter Moon in Aquarius.

This Moon phase occurs at 10.23 UTC.

November 5th, 6th - Taurids Meteor Shower.

The Taurids meteor shower runs yearly from September 7 to December 10. It peaks this year on the night of November 5.

November 11th - Rare Transit of the planet Mercury Across the Sun.

The planet Mercury moves directly between the Earth and the Sun. This is a rare event that occurs only once every few years. The next transit of Mercury does not take place until 2039.

November 12th - Full Moon in Taurus.

The November full Moon is on the opposite side of the Earth as the Sun, and its face will be fully illuminated. This phase occurs at 13:36 UTC. This full moon is known as Full Beaver Moon as this was the time of year beaver traps were used. It is also known as the Frosty Moon and the Hunter's Moon.

November 17th, 18th - Leonids Meteor Shower.

The Leonids meteor shower runs yearly from November 6-30. The Leonids meteor shower peaks this year on the night of the 17th and morning of the 18th.

November 19th – Last Quarter Moon in Leo.

This Moon phase occurs at 21.11 UTC.

November 20th - Mercury Retrograde ends in Scorpio.

You can now move forward with any delayed plans that you have been putting off due to the Mercury Retrograde phase. Relationships should soon improve as tensions ease.

November 24th - Conjunction of Venus and Jupiter.

A conjunction of Venus and Jupiter is visible on November 24. The two planets are within 1.4 degrees of each other in the night sky.

November 26th - New Moon in Scorpio.

This phase occurs at 15:06 UTC. This is an excellent time to view galaxies and star clusters because there is no moonlight visible.

November 28th - Mercury at Greatest Western Elongation.

The planet Mercury obtains western peak elongation of 20.1 degrees from the Sun.

NOVEMBER HOROSCOPE

NOVEMBER WEEK ONE

There may be a little bit of confusion and uncertainty around you at the current time, but you are absolutely strong enough to deal with it. As you re-evaluate your life, you are given a burst of reliable energy to move forwards with which will help you decide on the correct course of action. While you are not sure of your destination at the moment, gaining insight into your true feelings will help provide you with the clarity you seek. You may be feeling as if you are a little lost this week, and are left to walk alone in the dark guided only by your intuition and inner light. Focus on letting go of any mental blocks or negativity and allow your intuition to guide you. You have decisions to make in regards to broadening your horizons or staying in your comfort zone, you can have faith that you will make the correct decision.

NOVEMBER WEEK TWO

This week the planet Mercury makes a rare transit across the Sun. As it moves between the Sun and the Earth, it fires up consciousness, and you sweep away that which no longer serves you. Faced with a crossroads, this tells you to slow down and reflect. Downshifting and giving yourself time to focus on the correct direction enables you to head towards a goal post which is in alignment with your most authentic self. Striving for balance in your emotions allows you to nourish relationships, it draws a sense of well-being and equilibrium into your world. People are drawn to your energy, you inspire others, revealing a talent for healing. You make a difference in their world, the way you touch others with your nurturing spirit is inspiring. You are advised to look out for an event on the horizon as this gathering is meant for you. It is able to resolve stress and renewing your spirit. As an incredible opportunity for healing is coming your way, do get involved in mingling with other kindred spirits

NOVEMBER WEEK THREE

You begin the process of clearing up old emotions that have been cluttering up your life. It's through this process that you will be able to find the clarity that you have been looking for. Consider this as a help for you to find the direction you are seeking. Time is needed to find the clear path forward. Doing this inner work enables you to go through a time of evaluation. There may have been some difficulties in your life, and you may have felt as though things have been confusing. You are urged to put aside issues over which you have no control and focus instead on matters over which you can assert positive change. You will start to feel far more in control and begin to feel lighter and revitalized as a result. This the start of a new chapter of potential. There are many layers to be revealed, as it draws a sense of warmth and abundance into your world.

NOVEMBER WEEK FOUR

You may have emotional baggage which is hindering your progress. Heading in this direction puts the focus on creating stability, equilibrium, and steady resources. Once you obtain a stable base, your thoughts will turn to matters of the heart. It does suggest that there is terrific potential possible with a flexible and patient outlook. This is a slow burning situation which matures over time. There will be an opportunity to get involved in progressing a venture which holds significant meaning to you. This is a time where significant change is possible, you prepare to embark on a path which is rewarding and enlightening. As you take great strides to understand the elements which surround you, you become involved in higher development. You are introspective on this contemplative journey. Obstacles and hurdles are no match for your determined spirit.

DECEMBER ASTROLOGY

December 4th – First Quarter Moon in Pisces.

This Moon phase occurs at 06.58 UTC.

December 12th - Full Moon in Gemini.

The Moon is on the opposite side of the Earth as the Sun, and its face will be fully illuminated. This moon phase occurs at 05:14 UTC. This full moon is known as the Full Cold Moon because this is when chilly winters air arrives and nights become long and dark. This full moon is also known as the Long Nights Moon and the Moon Before Yule.

December 13th, 14th - Geminids Meteor Shower.

The Geminids meteor shower runs each year from December 7-17. The Geminids meteor showers peaks this year on the night of the 13th and morning of the 14th.

December 19th – Last Quarter Moon in Virgo.

This Moon phase occurs at 04.57 UTC.

December 22nd - December Solstice.

The 2019 December solstice occurs at 04:19 UTC. The South Pole of the earth tilts toward the Sun, which, having reached its most southern place in the sky, is directly over the Tropic of Capricorn at 23.44 degrees south latitude. This December solstice also marks the first day of winter (winter solstice) in the Northern Hemisphere.

December 21st, 22nd - Ursids Meteor Shower.

The Ursids meteor shower occurs each year from December 17 - 25. This meteor event peaks this year on the night of the 21st and morning of the 22nd.

December 26th - New Moon in Capricorn.

This moon phase occurs at 05:15 UTC. This is an excellent time to view galaxies and stars because there is no moonlight visible.

December 26th - Annular Solar Eclipse.

An annular solar eclipse occurs because the Moon is too far away from the Earth to adequately hide the Sun. This results in a ring of light around the dark Moon. The Sun's corona is not visible during an annular eclipse.

DECEMBER HOROSCOPE

DECEMBER WEEK ONE

Events on the horizon speak of sunshine arriving, you are hungry for new experiences and eager to expand your horizons. Breaking free of restrictions, you open the door to an enticing venture which holds plenty of promise. This satisfies your need for creativity and innovation, your curious mind is stimulated and engaged in developing this potential. It is likely to offer you many gifts which lead to further progress over time. You can expect serendipity to follow you wherever you go this week, events arrive to fill your days with excitement. Focusing on developing an area which is meaningful to you will provide you with beautiful results. There is enticing energy coming which gives you plenty of opportunities to see improvement in your circumstances. The more you stir the pot of creativity, the more potent a brew you are mixing, leading to inspired ideas and goals.

DECEMBER WEEK TWO

It is a beneficial time to expand your horizons, broadening your scope of potential does draw wonderful experiences into your life. Minor frustrations soon give way to events of great importance. Increased activities spark heightened creativity, this will hold you in good stead over the coming weeks. You are drawing gain into your life, this is an important journey which sees you highly optimistic and happy about developing a significant situation. Completing all the details sets the stage for stable growth. As you broaden your scope you bring in new influences which calibrate your talents, this all leads to excellent gifts being developed. The more you hone your skills, the more success you can expect.

DECEMBER WEEK THREE

There will be plenty to look forward to over the next little while. This direction takes you towards a time where you can feel more appreciated. Your inspiration is fueled by a sense of security and abundance which arrives to bolster your spirits. You enter a productive time which sends you trailblazing towards realizing a significant goal. Your creativity is peaking with fresh sparks to be developed. You can trust that life becomes lighter and more manageable soon. You will have the chance to reconnect with your passions. An increase in social invitations provides you with several memorable occasions. If an opportunity for a group project crosses your path, you can go for it. It's likely to develop into a lively endeavor. As you look out on the vision of your dreams there is much to look forward to, allow your inspiration and motivation to propel you forward towards the realization of your goals.

DECEMBER WEEK FOUR

Your personal life holds a surprising twist as you find the path ahead opens unexpectedly. This places you in the front seat to capitalize on the potential possible. No longer dreaming about the future, you can tackle a plan of action and embrace creatively developing a more profound bond with another who captivates your heart. This allows you to express your playful side, communications are highlighted as being fundamental to this process. Personal growth, life changes, rebooting and revamping your own life all enable you to make substantial progress. A wake-up call arrives to improve your confidence, it leads you towards a time where you focus on developing romance and passion in your life. This highlights the potential possible, you are committed to achieving your personal goals, this puts the spotlight on a significant situation which holds substantial promise in your life.

Dear Reader,

I hope you have enjoyed planning your year with the stars utilizing Astrology and Zodiac influences. Twelve zodiac star sign books are released each year which detail a monthly list of astrological events, and a weekly (four weeks to a month) horoscope. You can find me on my Facebook page:

https://www.facebook.com/Siasoz

Feedback is welcomed and appreciated.

Many Blessings,

Sia Sands

Made in the USA
Lexington, KY
07 December 2018